Women Of Honoring

A Dedication And Tribute Towards ALL Women

Robert McLearren

authorHOUSE®

AuthorHouse™
1663 Liberty Drive
Bloomington, IN 47403
www.authorhouse.com
Phone: 1 (800) 839-8640

Published by AuthorHouse 08/28/2017

ISBN: 978-1-5462-0673-6 (sc)
ISBN: 978-1-5462-0674-3 (e)

CONTENTS

TO MY SWEET FRIEND

I think of her all the time, she is a joy to talk to, a lady who's at the ready, a friend to mend a broken heart that once was torn apart.

I am happy she chose me because we can be more of a solid friendship that won't be kept to ourselves as we together shout it out loud in front of the vast crowd that no shrowed will cover as we soon discover

... what we mean, to each other.

SOMEWHERE

Babe, you are here ... somewhere ... out there. In an ocean of the vast seas someday we'll be together and become as one two can be.

Swim strong, swim might, I will be here day and night. Your heart as my guiding light, I won't give up my line nice and tight, I need you to regain my direction of sight ... I shall look for you, that's all I can do, as you swim far or near one thing to me is very clear ...

We belong in each other's hearts of our very own ... atmosphere.

SWEET DISTRACTION

There she is, always there for me wanting to be ... my friend. I can't ask for more when she has so much in store. She's my friend, my angel of respect as she happens to direct her care and love upon me.

I dearly miss this attention from a sweet distraction as she takes away the pieces of fractions from my life and replaces it with warmth and satisfaction without the daily strife.

She is what I've been looking for on my road towards gold, she shines ever so bright ... as she becomes ... my guiding light

YOU ONCE WERE MINE.

We've been together for a long time, now I'm going to have to call you, you once were mine. The many days we shared together always shined, now I'm going to have to call you, you once were mine.

The love, the sweetness, the cherished completeness, now I'm going to have to call you, you once were mine. The joy, the sorrow of reaching for another tomorrow, now I'm going to have to call you, you once were mine.

The pain of your strain as you try to regain of wanting to refrain from the straps of this world that kept you under raps for so long now, I must learn to let you go, somehow.

As we together say good-bye with tears in our eyes, as we shout out as we cry ... You are mine!

KNOCKED OFF MY FEET

I couldn't believe my eyes, did I just die and had seen an angel or did I come to and saw you in a different angle?

All just the same, your name IS an angel. An angel of sweetness, kindness and forgiveness. An angel has all this and more, from a brilliant bright of light captured my sight and turned night into day.

A woman with so much to say ... without saying a word, she is silent yet strong, she's always there to help you along.

She's caring and unique, someone to cherish as ones life is complete. She's my friend, she's my angel, my guardian without even trying ... she touched my heart and I am amazed ... I'm not even dying.

I CAN'T LET GO

Here you are on our bed, tears from your eyes flow down your head, this was the day I've always dread to have to let you go, I wish it was me instead.

We had alot of years together, we've faced all kinds of weather, from the rain we would refrain and from the light of the sun we had our fun turning the clocks back when we were twenty-one.

Your heart is so close to mine, the only thing I regret is just a matter of time. How can I hold a memory in my arms? You've always gave me your love, never harm, your sweetness and your charm ...

Please tell me, how can I let you go? As your love for me flows from your eyes down the sides of your face how can I replace a love ... as yours? Your heart pours with deep feelings as I try to comfort you with my greetings. I thank God for you and everything that you do because with out you ... there is no me, to be, complete ...

I still can't let go.

HOW CAN I SPEAK TO HER?

I'm a wreck! How can I expect to talk with her? I see her very clear and yet she's so far away. What am I going to do? What am I going to say? What are the correct words to be gathered here today?

I need her in my life, to end my sorrow and the strife and maybe one day ... make her become my wife! She is what I need to be more of a me as two can be!

She is a gift that gives my life lift as she shifts into high gear while showing me no fear as one thing is clear, she's happy to be near a new friend who happens to lend as he extends his hand who wants to help her from the waters on to dry land.

How can I make her understand the kind of man ... I am?

THE WARMTH OF KNOWING YOU

How do you do it? Each and every day without using words to say choosing feelings that fly through the ceiling and above the clouds shouting out loud over the crowds below.

"We're in love!" You have shown to be disguised as a sweet dove spreading our love from coast to coast, I never knew that this is the highest you ever flew! The warmth of knowing you is all the love that you give and seeing it through ... there's nothing more that you can do.

Just keep doing what you do best because in my eyes, you've already had passed the test - without having to guess as we're together unified and blessed.

I love you and thank God we are two ... as one can do.

I LOVE HAVING YOU AROUND

I love having you around, painting the town up and down while standing together on solid ground. There is no other love to be found as I love having you around.

You are always sunny as it rains, you always find a way to begin again as you take life in, how do you prove it as you go through it?

When your loving all of us with your friendship and trust what is it that makes you smile even if it's just a little while?

"I just do what I must!"

"I enjoy life! Not the daily strife and I also love my friends in this small town and I too love - having you around."

WHERE COULD SHE BE?

I've looked high and low I just don't know where to go, even though I've seen her everywhere, she's still not here. I tell myself don't lean on fear because if I allow it, it will become clear as my search continues someday she'll be near.

As the day approach I will make the most of everything that I can, I'm not my biggest fan as I search for you from the water I hope to find you one day on dry land.

I am lost because the cost is so great from this long and extensive wait. Where could she be? If she could only be ... with me.

FROM THE LIGHT TOWER

From the light tower as I have showered all my love for the search of you, there's not much that I can do. From my boat as I float I throw my nets but all I seem to get is heartache and despair.

They say "there's plenty of fish in the sea!" How can that be? I keep casting and its' always ever lasting as time is continuing passing.

"Is there someone out there?" As I shout over the water, there's no reply as I cry ... when will this end? Will I have a lover or a friend? Will I have a heart or a stone?

Because honestly ... I no longer want, to be alone.

I NEED HER

Women will always have a heart because they do their part each and every day! You say what makes them this way? They care as they share that no one else can compare.

Once you've found her, don't let her go, she will show how her love grows as it flows ... to you. Be sure not to rush her, you will crush her if you go too fast. Go slow and make it last and one day she will ask "would you like to be with me?"

Your heart will talk as it makes a spark in her heart making a light from the dark. This all could – happen one day as I continue to say ...

I need her.

HER HEART

Her heart is the best part, what she gives, she lives and shows every day. Its' in her way as she stays by me. Is it possible that we could be the joy that you and I share that can be declared a unified – union that only two people can be.

As she wakes each morning taking life in she does it without a grin or a frown because she's never down, always smiles with length that measure more than a mile.

How can this be done? While enjoying life and having fun. She does it with her heart and that is ...

the best part!

GOING TO THE DANCE

This lady I am with is filled with love and romance I'm looking forward to our dance. As we do, two become one. She is a joy, a sweetness of fun. We hold each other tight as we continue to dance through the night.

The music is playing as we're swaying while in my mind I'm praying that this lady tonight can make everything alright just from her care and self will, her strong might. She is beautiful sweet and warm I'm looking forward to take her home.

As we look into each other's eyes there is no other place on earth I would rather be. I am happy she chose me, she is my best friend with a warm heart that knows no end.

THE SEARCH

As my heart is sinking, I can't help thinking I may never find you. Time has come and gone, I can't even sing a song knowing that your out there instead of along. Where may you be? Am I still able to see just how much you mean to me?

Your amongst a million of fish that I wish to dish up. What is the right bait? To elaborate, to make things straight in my life as you become my first mate.

It will be great when the search is over, I won't have to feel that I've sailed to the white cliffs of Dover!

PLEASE DON'T GO

When we met, you were heaven sent. My eyes could never leave your face as you had graced your presence in the room ... Please don't go. After a while, you made me smile, held me close and made the most of what we could together ... Please don't go. We began a wonderful friendship, one without end, a joy to this very day that I can't put into words to say ... Please don't go. Now, you became my wife and had fulfilled my life, with love and sweetness, without sorrow and inner tearness ... Please don't go.

I'm much older now, with your love beside me, cherished and complete, we came far, we did defeat, all obstacles in our way ... Please don't go. As I hold your hand, before I cross into the beautiful promised land, together we understand of what we have ... I have you in my heart and soul, I will never let you go, with my final breath before I rest, there is something I must get off my chest ... I will always love you ... Please, don't let go.

A NIGHT OUT AT DINNER

All women have a heart, all women have a soul, if you love them and hold them tight, they will never let you go. A ladies feelings flow deep because she knows, when loved and caressed, she becomes YOUR best on the same runway you both share with NO ONE to compare as they all look at you ... and stare.

While the stars shine bright above, its' because of you and your love. Makes me want to fly away ... with my sweet loving dove.

MY FUTURE LADY LOVE

My future lady love is flying somewhere up above, as I continue to wait for her to land, I just want to be there for her hand.
As the sand flows through time would she one day consider to be mine?

I have loved women all my life, they are treasures without the loneliness of strife. I'd loved to be married and be carried by her love but for now, only she possess.

She has the cure for loneliness and a love that always endures, sweet and pure. Only one question remains, will she ever land? Not only so that I can take her hand ... I'd like to be able to capture her heart which happens to be the best part!

TOGETHER

When we're together I feel like kids, doing everything like we once did. Going to the movies at half price, those times were so very nice! Swimming at the lake and acting goofy, we were kids free and loosely.

We had fun in the sun and we're no longer as one. The love for our youth is done, while a new life together has begun, time to time we do reflect back upon our fun as the love for each other will never be gone.

They say hold on tight its' going to be a bumpy ride, for us those days are over. Only love remains inside.

I FELL FOR YOU

What did you do to my heart? You held it close and made a spark while never tearing it apart, how are you able to do this with love and care as your feelings are everywhere. There's so much that you share that you can be declared your not going nowhere.

I'm very thankful that you were found, I was lost at a heavy cost now I'm going forward bound. With you by my side we'll make the journey while we take that ride. State by state as we evaluate the miles that make us smile.

I fell for you but not with heavy lumps, sweet beats from every thump of my heart.

MAY I FOLLOW?

Where are you going? May I follow? You have a heart I'd like to be apart. I am a nice man never shallow ... may I follow? I have seen as you allow others' to lean on you, seam to know what to do.

As you invite everyone in can I also be your friend? ... May I follow? A woman who's in front of the band always glad to extend her hand. She's always there floating on water or standing on sand, she's a friend rescuing you onto dry land.

Just enter into my arms as I free you from all harm sharing my love is the charm which also can be the very key ... to me.

WOMEN ARE BEAUTIFUL

Women are beautiful! They see with their feelings while believing, if you touch their heart in the rightful manner, you won't have to worry about them changing the channel.

Treat them like treasure that no one else can measure, love them and hold them tight and you'll be together with them day and night. Allow them to shine bright, so that you can be blinded by their beautiful sight ... love them and respect them as your listening to their sweet tone ...

... then you will know, you won't be alone.

ALL IN THE MATTER AND
THE MEANING OF TIME

On the day that I find you I will shout out and cry there is love between you and I! With the sky of blue, you are for me and I am for you there's nothing we can't do ... together.

Lean on me and soon you'll be in a better state of mind as you will find that my love for you is warm, sweet and kind.

We're in each others' hearts, you gave me life and a new fresh start. Your very good to me because I happen to be what you gave ... lives inside of me as I had saved.

You've shown me love because you are there, your sweetness and your care are always shared by you as you give unselfishly of who you are as you live your life along with mine. Its' all in the matter and the meaning ... of time.

MEASURING YOUR LOVE

There isn't an ounce of your love that you keep to yourself its' for all to see never gets put on a shelf.

As it rises it surprises me on how much you have to share. It is great how you can communicate with another, take their heart and make it a part of your own.

Some hearts are made of stone, sometimes they are alone in hopes to find someone ... as they stare at the phone. As you shake the batter, you ask them "what's the matter?"

Don't worry, I am here holding your hand and being near, I'm your friend, please have no fear. One thing is clear with your love we all have something ... to cheer!

WHAT A WOMAN SHE IS

What a woman she is, giving her time like it was mine, being warm and kind, wanting to be accepted, never neglected ... in a world that can be sometimes cold.

Watch as she slowly unfolds, her truth be told as she gives her love and care just by wanting to be there. "What did I do to deserve her friendship as she never leaves my side?" I'm filled with pride and respect, there's nothing she would expect, except the very same in the end from her very own ... friend.

WHERE ARE YOU GOING?

"**W**here are you going?" "I'm going to look for my friend." She's out there somewhere ...

... near or far in her house or outside in her car, she too is looking, hopefully ... for me. If only she could see what's inside of me, she would know as I happen to show just how much she means to me.

GOING THE EXTRA MILE

What is a friend? She is real who can feel with her heart and places you in a special part that no one else has, her very existence is to care for you as you already do ... for her.

Going the extra mile while she smiles knowing that your friends. God makes each of us special ... I think women are a little more, they have love, they have sweetness and plenty more in store as we open the door for them ... they open their hearts ... and let us in with acceptance and a smile, never a grin.

Be honest with her that's all she asks, she's not going to give you a series of tasks. She'll always be your friend ... just be sure, never to hurt her ... in the end or you too will suffer as well my friend.

MY JOY OF KNOWING YOU

The joy of knowing that you are there is a gift that can't be compared, your an original, one of a kind, a friend that's hard to find.

No one is like you, your brand new just like on the day you were born, you were sent from heaven, your wings untorn as you landed here on earth as a baby angels birth. The joy you have giving to all of us, your friendship, your trust is what you felt you must just by being there for ALL of us!!

Don't ever despair, you don't realize the size of touch you have impacted on all of us!! One life touches another, please don't feel the hurt or the pain, I promise, with friends ... you'll be able to live ... again.

FRIENDS

I find it to be true because our friendship happens to be you, its' in all the things that you do, you are there wanting to care and sometimes unaware what you do for others, like a sister or a brother.

We all have hearts to follow as we do our part. We comfort and we guide to help he or she inside. The pain can be intense but if you could hold my hand, it can be washed away and rinsed.

Start a new brand of clean and do what you mean by having fun in the sun instead of gloom alone inside an empty room, be amongst friends, you'll be without end as we happen to lend our hand to you in return.

Don't allow your heart to burn, retaliate as you already appreciate what your friends have to offer you because ... it's in everything ... that you do.

ARE YOU A DREAM
OR REALITY?

As I dream I see your face out of many dreams I could dream, this is one I don't want to replace. From your contours I could trace a new love I can embrace.

Wait, your only a dream it seams, could this be one day a reality for you and I? Could we try as we cry for our love to never die?

Let's not question as we happen to mention on how we're going to one day meet.

We'll have love take over as I search for you, that's what I'm going to do.

Never give up, never give in I will dream of you while I'm awake and never close my eyes

... again.

I'M NOT A FISHERMEN

Each day I go to the lake make no mistake, you are out there as I'm waiting for you to take the bait.

Many Fish to wish upon I just need one to carry on.

You are not my trophy this is true all I want is to love you, I continue to wait day and night hoping our eyes find its' sights.

I need you, what am I going to do without you? Do you know? If you do please show. I'm out here getting bit and sun burned when all I want is to have you in my life and home.

If you know please show ... I need your love to flow.

CLOSER

Get closer please don't be shy I love the twinkles in your eyes, as you draw near you approach having no fear.

You are sweet and warm you don't feel you have to perform the feelings you disguised as greetings during our meeting.

It seemed we traveled far as we got into our car, to leave the world behind in search of a new place, a new find.

We will miss our friends and family, we just need to be closer to begin our journey

... as our hearts intertwine our love is now together

For all time.

TOGETHERNESS

Togetherness is a joyful bliss. Togetherness is even though were old we can be kids. Having you by my side is wonderful to know how much you show our togetherness together.

We are a couple that's made of two, one will be alone and three will be a croud. Let us be happy and proud as we shout out to the world good and loud.

Our love will stand for others' to understand what a man has for a woman and a woman for a man.

HURTING

Hurting is the pain, do you feel the same? Would you like to get together out from underneath this cloud of bad weather?

Let's start again this time you and I as we put back the sparkles in our eyes, we now have a life that will never die because we know each other and we'll do more than try.

It's wonderful to see the smile on your face, now replaced from the cries you once had in your eyes. Your love is strong you will have it for now on.

Please lean on me, together we will see the sun and no more hurting from the pain we both used to rely on ... from the strain.

AM I STARING?

I'm sorry, I don't mean to stare, I am lost and you are found while standing there. Your eyes take me away during your existence of your beautiful way.

I'm glad your here today I just wish I could find the words to say, what is the warmth your looking for so that I can be with you and adore what your life means to me.

Can we see what kind of togetherness we can be?

DON'T GO

For as long as we both shall live we have so much to give, we will always have love to show just please don't go.

You have a way that shines everyday, in your walk, in your style even it's just for a little while.

As your standing there never demanding where we two can cherish each others' hearts being a part of a unified union.

Please don't go.

THE LOSS

The cost of a loss is full of pain, you don't have to run away, someday you'll be able to regain a life to start again.

It's going to take time soon you will be able to find a person who's loving and kind.

Please don't get mad even though you have the right to be sad. This is the time to grieve, in your heart he's never going to leave.

Hold on tight to his memory, when your kids grow up you'll have a story on how you two had met I know your never going to forget the love you both once shared ...

Only now it's in your heart to be shared as you care for someone ... out there.

MY KEEPS?

In my sleep I wonder if I could keep the joy and love I don't ever want to lose from above. As I dream I happen to see this lovely lady before me, may I keep your heart, your love and soul? If this wasn't a dream I sure wouldn't let you go.

Please don't be surprised because in your eyes I see me, going to places with you only the two of us can do.

YOU ARE BEAUTIFUL!

When we go out there's no doubt you are beautiful! You don't need to question before we reach our destination as you happen to mention, "Do I look alright tonight?"

Holding you in my arms loving your sweetness and charm, no cause for alarm. There's no maybe baby I am crazy about you!

There is nothing wrong with you, nothing more that one can do when it happens to be you, your already loving and true.

THE LIGHTHOUSE

Do you see the bright light up ahead amongst those trees? Could it be that we found our way in the dark free from harm of any sharks? Don't despair, we're almost there ...

The help we need will be everywhere. We are no longer lost, we are found by the people themselves that live in this little town.

Be happy, it's time to celebrate! The waves and the current won't decide our fate all because of a lighthouse that guided our way so that we may be able to live ...

another day.

> You are my light
> tonight ... I love you!

TAKING NOTES

On the day we met, I couldn't believe I had let you once slip away to this very day I regretted that way without the words to say.

I can't help thinking that you were taking notes as I wanted to devote every minute with you. There was no way you could know because I've never showed how much you meant to me.

I want to pass the test because I can only guess what I could happen to miss ... your love, your kiss and never ending bliss.

YOUR GUIDE

If you should decide please allow me to be your guide while we take the ride through life with you by my side.

It won't always be fun, together we're never done. Sometimes it can be rough we stand tall, we are tough ...

Nothing will get in our way, today or any other day. We will never get stuck from the oil slicks and the muck because we won't need luck ... our love will stampeed through life's games of pain ...

as we will always happen to rise up once again!

ALONE OR THE PHONE

My arms are wide to hold you inside to keep you from harm and suicide. Your heart won't break because your in heavy pains and aches try to calm yourself, you don't need to shake ...

Someone is already here for you and you know what to do, take comfort, take shelter no need for Helter Skelter.

Your heart is not made of stone you don't have to be alone just please ... pick up the phone and someone will see you home.

NOTE TO SELF

Note to self, I need to get out of my head and think of only of her instead. If I'm trying to impress, I need to stop the wrong address ... trying to reach her heart with love and respect and keeping myself centered without the strong direct.

She speaks to me without words, she's in my heart, that she knows no part, not even a spark or a hint of a feeling from a dent

It can be said she was heaven sent but I keep hitting the wall instead.

NO LONGER ASLEEP

I need to wake up and see just how much women mean to me. I've been alone for far too long I can no longer go on.

What is my fate if I don't have my mate? The future seems grim but only if you could let me in, together we may ... win!

If I can only find you and recognize the things you can do maybe I can get through and be able to touch your face, have your love ... your sweet grace.

You manage to place your warmth upon my heart, because of this you're giving us a beautiful brand new start!

LET ME TAKE AWAY
YOUR TEARS

Allow me to take away your tears, shed you from your fears so that you can get near.

I'm here for you, to do what you need me to do, to help you with any task ... all you have to do ... is ask.

Please don't put on a mask to hide from me, I won't be able to see how great your needs are to be.

There is a woman in front of me who is hurt from the dirt of her past ... but you know, it won't last because your love will carry on, it will surpass anything that comes in your path.

ARE WE THERE YET?

You can surely bet, are we there yet? Yes we are, as you put your hand into mine it's just a matter of time that your heart will follow.

Don't let your pain weep and wallow take a new lane and drain your sorrow as you look for a brand new tomorrow with a new man who wants to understand the woman you want to be.

Please believe me as we see the sun rise, no more tears in your eyes followed by the cries as you once had shout ...

"Is there any love out there? Because I'm beginning to doubt, from being alone I have to much of an amount!"

The joy we both now share is in our hearts spans and spreads everywhere.

Come, look and stare, we don't care ... your a witness as we ourselves have experienced love and inner completeness!

Are we there yet? Oh yes! The roads have finally had merged as we splurge of a life we now share ...

together.

I BOUGHT YOU A PUPPY

Today I bought you a puppy, cute and fluffy and a bit chubby. Friendly as can be as you already see.

Playful and joyful he could be a handful! Jumping around up and down, this pup is going to town!

Be sure to take him out because they're won't be any doubt as how excited he can be as he runs about!

This little guy can eat but please don't give him any treats he still has a vast amount of dog food below at his feet.

With his love you'll happen to meet, he's soft and sweet and a real treat!

YOUR GIFTS

Your a woman of many gifts because you yourself happen to lift those that feel they have none.

They are alone, you come along singing your song giving your friends hope as they try to cope while focusing on their scope.

Some friends think they are going to stay this way as you change their life they live in from night into day. By the way did you happen to say the heart you give every day?

Without words unselfishly you share your love and care your always there with no one to compare.

I CAN'T LOSE YOU

Your a beautiful painting without any paint, your an angel that's already a saint, you have a love you share without restraint all because you care just by being there.

I can't lose you, I wouldn't know what to do because I'll won't be able to see things through without you.

What will the future hold if we couldn't watch our lives together unfold?

What I'm about to say may be bold but this must be told ... your my woman, my love, my wife ...

I can't live without you ... your my whole life!

I'M NOT GOING TO
SAY GOOD NIGHT

Please come close because your the most I could ever need, we are free from the search it is now over, we won't even need a four leaf clover.

As I hold you tight I'm not going to say good night we are staying together past the dawn and from then on.

In front of me, here you stand, can I be your loving man? Will you accept or deny? All I want to be is your guy, what I ask isn't much as I long for your touch.

Please don't go allow me to show you what's in my sight. I'm not going to say good night.

Printed in the United States
By Bookmasters